The Country Gambler

For Lewis,
in the English Lakes
(Rydal, 2019)

Erica McAlpine

Erica McAlpine

The
Country
Gambler

Shearsman Books

First published in the United Kingdom in 2016 by
Shearsman Books
50 Westons Hill Drive
Emersons Green
BRISTOL
BS16 7DF

Shearsman Books Ltd Registered Office
30–31 St. James Place, Mangotsfield, Bristol BS16 9JB
(this address not for correspondence)

www.shearsman.com

ISBN 978-1-84861-481-9

Contents

for my parents

Sempervivum

Long-living plant, that flowers on the ground and
spawns in circles round itself, whose low and quiet
center stores a gravity not surpassed by
stone, down to the pith,

and that waits on no sustenance, but still feeds
on both drought and faith, put forth into these leaves,
as with a new rosette, your not-quite-pink teeth,
your feather-white breath.

1

These are the Happiest Days

Miami

Under this canvas cabana, white bower
of unadulterated hope, I won't tell
you these are the happiest days we'll ever
pass. Best not to say.

Nothing will come and steal from us this hour
unless it's our nagging, aggravating will
to think of things always as worse than they are,
to cloud up the day,

as it were. Otherwise, it's in our power
to spend the whole afternoon drinking our fill
of sun (soaking now through the canvas over
us) and even say

what's on our minds a little. Because showers
do come (look at Cornelia and Raphael –
just one second and she's lost him forever).
It's the normal way

of things to bloom and brighten, then turn sour.
We haven't been singled out – we're not *bad* souls.
But happiness rarely stays in place. These are
the happiest days.

The Poet's Prayer

after Horace Odes 1.31

What should the poet say here at Apollo's
new temple? What should he ask for, pouring new
wine from the bowl? Not Sardinia's harvests
or Calabria's

herds; not gold or ivory from the East; not
even for that countryside where the gentle
river Liris grips the earth with her silent
thread. The gods decide

which farmer gets to trim his vines with the best
Calenian blades, which merchant gets to drain
golden chalices of wine just now traded
for Syrian wares.

(A man *must* be held dear if he can, three or
four times every year, suffer, uninjured,
the Atlantic.) I grow olives and endives
and tender mallow:

give to me only what I am ready for,
a healthy heart, and a good mind, so that I
may spend my final days living free from shame
playing my lyre.

Marine Display

Blessed with his six jumbo-sized shoulders, the land
hermit crab knows the art of the hunch, which he
performs modestly so as to shuttle high
parts he can't let touch

the ground (a curved, fragile-skinned abdomen and
such). It is no wonder, with all that body
tucked up in his shell, that those buttress-shaped thighs
can't step but to clutch.

Needing grip is something we all understand,
who carry with us often quite a heavy
load on feet that are prone to trip, which is why
we love him so much.

The Country Gambler

You'll find me in the clover patch from August
to October, detangling tangled stem from stem,
inspecting each one over, knowing three
seems four when two stems meet and send a leaf
from under, or if they cross along the neck then
six can be the number. And some are tall,
and bent with rain, and overtop the grass,
while others, tiny, clump their leaves in bunches
thick as moss. (Once, I found a crumpled
one I'd flattened underfoot; discovering
it was lucky, I pressed it in a book.) Though
shade can turn the leafage blond, and wind
can push the petal-ends to ground and make them
hard to sort, I wouldn't cut the searching short.
Nothing's better than the luck you find.

An Opportunity

Strolling one morning on a stony
Greek volcano made once again habitable
by the sea, an agile, slender-framed cat,
a grey and feral-mouthed stray,
stopped above a wall of plaster-white
and settled upright there to look about
the shore, with a twitch inside his ear
and a lick across his maw, when from
above him on the bluff, a swallow
dove across his sight – he leaned
and swiped the bird from flight,
all instinct and speed and desire for plunder,
as though flying were no inimitable deed,
and a bird no thing to cower under.

Kite

It's hard to say a word these days
without suggesting the opposite, too,
as though life itself might also be
a metaphor for life, in which no matter
what you see, it isn't really true.
I saw a kite – the bird – above
me in the park one big and windy
afternoon in New York in the summertime
just gliding on the air (and how I loved
him there!) until a gust of autumn came
and jerked him sideways on the wing
so that I saw that what I saw
had not been bird at all, but feathers,
glue, and string. Let me tell it
to you straight, tell you exactly what
I mean: if a man can make so well
a copy of a bird that only wind can prove
its form, then art's duplicity's
the same. The realer it is, the better.

Swiss Painters

Only one was good at trees; the other, rocks.
Except these, nothing else distinguishable
between them I found. But how well one's tawny
conifers did please,

that shone, as bright as deep, the keen brown of fox
fur worn around, and from their tops could tumble
down feather-foliage whose dark tapestry
would keep through the freeze,

being winter-bound and home to mountain hawks.
Splendid rocks were harder and gave him trouble.
They were left for the other, who faithfully
could paint with ease

the rough outcrop's fissure veins and glacier pocks.
With natural gifts, anything's possible.
Condescend, fair giver of these, to make me
good at rocks. Or trees.

To the Ammonite

Charmouth

Named by Pliny, after the ram's horn, whose coil
is wound but half as tight as yours (its being
spiral-shaped and keratin-formed), that self-built
shell in which you floored

a dozen tiny rooms in mother of pearl
would dangle from its lip your body fleeing,
sink or rise in water's swaying, roll and tilt
now back, now forward,

after which you sailed millennia in shale
through which this morning we all pored, agreeing
there had never been a snail in sea or silt
time had so adored.

Bucket

Given the choice between a plastic bucket
and a wooden ladder, I would choose bucket
every time. There just isn't any sense
in choosing ladder.

It's not about one of them being *better*.
Both let you climb, but only one holds water.
Let us just remember there are moments when
that really matters.

Love Poem as Ars Poetica

Because I am the dog who thought
her pain was a location, shuffling in
and out of rooms, trying to escape it,
it forever following along,

you stick with me everywhere – not
you, but the idea. We begin
with something big, water, or the wind, thinking we can shape it
before it all goes wrong.

2

September

I will tend
the garden, but
really I am
waiting

for autumn.
I'll go softly into
the house carrying
fire wood and strip

the beds of their
summer linens.
I am aware
I have a

skin
that petals. I'll
be subtle.
I'll say,

this morning
the shrub hills
roll like sun
over a woman's

shoulder.
The wheat fields
wear a dark, thick
stubble.

The Chase

1.

In the only lasting colour of a Roman
wall fragment,
                  Apollo plays harp to a figure
        we can't see.

His rumpled apron reaches
            me where it stumbles
                  past all traces of itself, gold

and red, dust crumbling out,
            wrapping the god way up there
below his right knee.

There is a golden thread on the harp.
It reaches
            down to the fabric

turning lavender, spinning
            into cloth. Lineaments
            get woven into linen.

Everything hardening to bronze,
bending, and two sceptres pointing up
            from below

where the crossbow
            hangs –

Apollo holds the instrument
in his golden hands.

2.

And the river has one daughter
and Apollo loves her.
                    You can see in
                    the dazzled tips of grain

how much he burns, and in the morning
when the parched fields lit
            by travellers' torches fan out,

scorching themselves until the rain comes.
She is strolling near the river-mouth,
        he watches from a grove. Up and
down the river-mouth

she moves.
Her eyes and her lips are such
that just to look

is not enough;
and the fingers of the hands of the wrists
and her bare arms tumbling
                            down

her shoulders, and as she flees,
the drifting far-
            off thunder.

The Fawn

after Horace Odes 1.23

My love eludes me like a fawn
frightened by dark foothills.
The wood is chilling. The wind
is falling. She hears her mother calling.

Sounds of spring shaking new in the foxgloves,
or pale, green lizards low on the bramble,
these lovely quivers in the trees and I
make her tremble.

Her knees buckle. Her heart quickens.
Quiet Chloe, your shiver
is lion's hair tickling a lion's back.
Leave your mother. Now you are a lover.

The Impatiens

The impatiens shakes its ruffled colour at
the wind. Let the maples measure grace. Twenty
purple lichens tingle on a stone. Through me
you have come and gone.

The maples let the wind through. Twenty ruffled.
Purple colour shakes on lichens. You measure
a stone, its grace gone, and tingle. Come have me
at the impatiens.

The lichens have measure. Gone the maples, the
wind. Twenty ruffled impatiens tingle on.
Let a stone come at its purple. You colour,
and grace shakes through me.

Old Woman with a Goitre

Just as in a field a herd of cows
will lean and clang their copper cauldrons
like the rain, with dawn breaking pink
upon their bangles, and stand there blotched,
humbled and hindered by their own sound,
and crumple their knees, dumbstruck,
while every jerk of their backs and involuntary
gesture registers the ringing of a bell,
so this old woman stood behind a mountain
spruce, struck by something in the field,
a row of phlox or patch of bluebell,
holding her spray of yellow gentians,
while that great ball shifted on her neck,
ripe as a stitch of loganberry.

To a Bull

after Horace Odes 2.5

That lovely neck of your young heifer
isn't ready, yet, to bear the yoke. She's never
had a mate before; she couldn't tolerate
the kind of weight you'd give her.

Her spirit's in the fields, where just now
you can see her splashing through a river;
to break the heat and play with other calves
beneath wet willow groves

she's especially eager. Don't crave
the unripe grape. Soon enough
for you will autumn's varied colors
paint those hanging clusters dark;

soon it's you your heifer
will be trailing. Defiant days are sailing
past – they'll give to her the years
they're taking now from you.

She'll seek a man as brave, as prized
as timid Pholoe isn't, nor Chloris,
though his shoulders are as white as moon-
beams on the sea, nor Gyges, who's

so finely featured, if you placed
him in a group of girls, he'd sure escape
the notice of his mates, disguised, as such,
by flowing hair and so ambiguous a face.

The Birthday

Because I had been hoping, the entire year,
only for you to remember, nothing more,
no belated bouquet or bending over
backward now will do.

Now, my fervent wish is just that I could swear,
this coming November, to settle the score.
But by autumn's blustery end, you'll be lover
again – and I, too.

A Request

after Horace Odes 3.26

I have lived my life as a capable man,
and of love's many battles won my share.
But today I am laying down
my weapons and my lyre

by the wall to the left of Venus di Mare.
Here are all my blazing torches,
and my axes, and my bows, that were
once such a threat to opposing forces.

Goddess, queen, you who keep
Memphis and mild Cyprus free from snow,
will you touch, with your lofty whip,
just once, the haughty Chloe?

Oaks

Oh palsied oak, oh barren branch, whose dwindled
arms still doggedly extend though cattle-torn
and broken at the shoots, whose trunk still bends to
winds, wet winter floods

may soak you end to end, but life would kindle
green inside these limbs now thin and weather-worn:
I've seen the sun on oaks, what beams it sends to
coax their pent-up buds.

The Sabine Jar

after Horace Odes 1.9

Do you see how Mount Soracte shines
in the distance, white under a mantle of snow?
Already now the trees cannot sustain their burdens.
The stream stands still with ice.

Let's dispel the cold – you pile
the wood high in the fireplace and I'll
take down that Sabine jar we
filled four years ago

and we'll stay indoors leaving
all to chance. As soon as the sea winds
quiet down, the cypress too will stop,
and our old mountain ash.

About tomorrow, never ask.
Each day's a gain. While you're
still young, don't scorn sweet loves
and dances:

each night in all the parks
and every city square there's secret
whispering in the dark at a certain hour,
and just now in the corner of some bar

there's a girl laughing while a gift is
slipping from her arm, or is it from her finger,
and she is only
pretending to resist.

3

Corinth

If we'd sailed here on a boat, and not this bus,
perhaps you could love – *we* could love together –
so blue a bay, tucked down under rocky hills,
and those salt-white bluffs.

But the place has wounded only one of us,
leaving a live horse and a hurt horse tethered.
Just moving the same way is hard; standing still's
also proving tough.

Above us, noisy gulls fuse and disperse, fuse
and disperse, or gather, and fly in feathered
unison over worn-out earth and sea-swells
suddenly turned rough.

The Middle Way

after Horace Odes 2.10

The right way is never to sail too far,
nor always to hug the tumbling shore
when storms are gathering –

for whoever finds pleasure in the middle way
humbly avoids the squalor of a house in shambles
and the grandeur of one inspiring envy –

the tallest pine sways easiest in the wind,
the highest towers fall heaviest, lightning
always seeks the tops of mountains.

The well-prepared heart has hope during
adversity and fear during prosperity since Jupiter
brings winter back as quickly as he

drives it away. Things are never bad
forever. Sometimes Apollo's lyre awakens
with song, sometimes it lies in slumber:

show spirit even on the worst days, and, likewise,
fold up your sails if they are swelling just now
under too fortunate a breeze.

June Gloom

Los Angeles

And still, the weather's calmer, brighter, better
here than where most people spend their summer days.
Morning mist dissipates soon, and the low cloud
cover; high noon paints

the sky blue. After sundown, a light sweater
will keep us warm if the marine layer lies
too close to shore again. I think that we should
refrain from complaints

of haze to those who've built homes where it's wetter,
or those with difficult lives, no matter why,
whether their forecast is grim or not. Dark moods
require restraint.

To bear, with equanimity, a letter
bringing the news of minor drought while sucked dry
and crying out, deserted, from cracked sands would
try the strength of saints.

Simple Things Are Best

after Horace Odes 1.38

I do not like a garland so fancily woven –
even a bough of lime bark is too garish.
So leave the last rose of summer
still blooming on the bush.

You are distinguished by the myrtle,
graced by the simplest flower,
you pouring and I too in myrtle drinking
under the bower.

Marriage

The yellow-breasted weaver's nest we found
suspended from our tree that second year
was finely built, but not as safe as it appeared,
for though it hung with leafage all around,
and far above the hazards on the ground,
instead of open at the top, and balanced
on the branches like a bowl, the entrance
was an under-sided hole that pointed down,
so if a gust should break a limb, or lightning
toss the nest and make it come untied,
the birds would have to cling onto its sides
(with tight-clenched feet and shining, frightened
eyes) while all the eggs they'd laid and sat
upon to hatch and prized go tumbling out.

Stanza

I'm not supposed to decorate your room.
Your father thinks it would be tempting fate,
that putting up the crib before the womb
has let its cargo down, early or late,
might set in motion something truly grim
from jealous gods, or ghosts importunate,
who watch, and who would punish me and him,
and that you could be lost. I'll have to wait.
I'll have to put away these dresses, too,
and store the matching pillows that I bought,
and say they are for friends and not for you,
and hope that fate is not privy to thought.
Unspoken thought gives license to enjoy
imagining a little girl. Or boy.

A Dedication

after Horace Odes 3.22

Guardian of these mountains, of these groves,
maiden goddess of all labouring girls,
Diana, who, called three times,
keeps death away while tri-formed,

this is your pine that hangs above
my roof, tree to which gladly
each year I'll give a boar
just now practicing sidelong thrusts.

Pond

Unembarrassed by sound, the geese dishevel
their plumes noisily and honk. Wherever they
waddle, they muddy. Never bottling up
anything they feel,

they spread it around for others to revel
in: worry, or jealousy, or joy. To bray,
both wings flapping, neck elongated, chinstrap
exposed, for a meal

seems, to them, wholly permissible. Their level
of transparency serves overall. Bury
your shame and suffer; say it loud and you keep
on an even keel.

Otherwise, everything – moulting, or travel,
flying sometimes for the full length of a day
without any idea of where to stop –
would be a big deal.

A Song for Lalage

LA-la-jee: Greek, "to prattle," after Horace Odes 1.22

When I am upright, and sure of love, I can
go anywhere, unarmed, whether the stormy
sands of the Southern Desert, or the swollen
ground freshly frozen

under, or the overwhelming rushes that
flood the famous Hydaspes river. Far past
the edges of my farm, deep in the Sabine
wood, I was singing

of Lalage, carefree and undefended,
when from the brush, a wolf – tougher than oak-fed
wolves from the North, lions bred on sandy plains –
upon seeing me,

fled (I was unafraid and alone). So put
me where no tree ever whispers, where no breeze
ever quickens to restore, where the clouds, thick
with thunder, send down

their lights, or in a land so scorched by sun no
man will build his home there, and still I will be
singing of my Lalage, sweetly laughing,
sweetly prattling.

Taking Charge

That fierceness doesn't guarantee you power.
Energized by the challenge, boldly throwing
his weight to push, still the ant can't move the stone.
Wrath won't make him large.

The best umbrella in a heavy shower
won't save your shoes – won't even keep from blowing
outside in. Sometimes there's nothing to be done:
you can't win. Emerge

from bed knowing you've got less than an hour,
brush, dress, grab the coat you've laid out for going
the night before, and find, again, that your phone
didn't take the charge.

Proof

after Horace Odes 1.34

Having been but a slight and infrequent
worshipper of the gods, and having roamed awhile,
expert in mistaken wisdom, today
I've been forced to set sail –

to renew a course I'd forsaken. You see,
Jupiter, who needs the clouds to throw
his lights, has driven, just now,
his clattering horses and chariot

through a clear blue sky,
so that the ground and the sea,
the river Styx's source and I
all were forcibly shaken. That's power –

enough to make high things low and low things
high, to humble the strong and lift the obscure.
From one man Fortune steals the crown;
on another she delights to place it.

4

The Sandhill Crane

When he decided to weather the early frosts,
and outstay fallen leaves all turned to mulch,
and graze our lawn in paces, with his neck
looped back, his head protruding forward,
both wings flapping over every step as if he were
a farmer driving a herd, shuffling stray things
into place, and always with his beak upturned,
like when a stifled feeling rises in the throat,
and one claw tucked up in his down at the sight of us
to pluck and preen and give his crown a shake,
we called it luck, his staying on to nest
among our pines (the dogwoods were out of season
but the pines were evergreen), so when he later
disappeared one cold December morning
filled with snow and ice, our best defence
was holding on to what we call migration,
that what is beautiful and gone has merely flown.

Denial

Because of their unfathomable distance
from us, and the slow yet unrelenting force
of light, which barrels on despite everything,
extinguished stars still

shine. As a result, all our gazing is chance.
Those old, bright forms – Orion's belt, the winged horse –
may well be gone by now, dark nothings, having
dazzled us their fill

and exploded. Years from now, by happenstance,
a child will notice something's missing, or worse,
won't, when the last beam of light stops appearing.
Imagine the thrill

astronomers must feel, knowing in advance
how long that news shall be belated. Their curse
is calculating loss but disbelieving
it, against their will.

Dragonfly

What would it do if it knew a blizzard was coming,
that there'll be snow underfoot tomorrow morning,

that the grasses that bind the river will all be frozen,
that the deer that step there will crack them,

that the stems themselves will die?
This insect thrums over the river through

the squat trees that lean from the fens,
its back the bluest blue, its vibratory wings,

swinging its weight among the bull-rushes...
In my dream the man I love is devoured

by lions before my eyes. I stand there lassoing
until he tells me to run away, and I run away.

Often what I think is beautiful in this world becomes so
beautiful in my mind that it dies. Why should my poem kill a
      dragonfly?

To Leuconoë

after Horace Odes 1.11

You should not ask
the gods what end
they've given you and me,
for it is wrong to know.

Nor should you ask
the stars. Better
to take things as they come,
whether there are many winters

left, or if this one
is the last, which just now
pounds the sea
on giant cliffs of stone.

If you are wise,
strain your wines and cut
short far-reaching hopes.
Life is brief –

as I speak the seconds go –
hold on to
day, think little
of tomorrow.

The Geraniums

Potted at night, not by you, the capable
gardener and once the blooming bride,
but by your black-thumbed, improbable
husband, a dutiful groom who tried
to keep them going when you weren't able,
hoping soon the surgeon's hand would slide
the hip back into place and hold it stable
long enough for you to heal on the inside
and save it from causing any more trouble,
and you would come home, rectified,
expecting all your purple cranesbills
to have wilted where you fell and dried,
only to find them blooming on the table
having never drooped and never died.

The Sharp Cold Dissolves

after Horace Odes 1.4

The sharp cold dissolves in spring and gentle winds.
At sea, the engines drag in all those dry ships.
The flocks have quit their stables, the ploughman's left
his hearth for meadows

no longer thread by frost. Under a full moon
Venus drives her choir, nymphs and graces loosen
the ground with their light, quick feet. The warming sun
is unfolding fields

in Sicily. Let's circle our heads with leaves
and flowers given to us by the opened
earth and in a shady grove offer the woods
a lamb or small goat.

Since death's impartial foot touches a pauper's
home the same as a king's, life's too short for long
hopes: night presses in, the old ghosts stir below
us, when we are gone

there will be no wine, no more slender girls to
look upon, not even Lycidas, who's just
now winning the heart of every man and
every woman.

An End

To fall out, to leave, as leaves falling out of trees.
The trees have rickety bones. The breeze is the jazz

rustling out of one. We are waiting for the leaves to hit
the ground. Nothing fastens them to the wind

unfastening the bright ones first. We don't say, *this winter
our plans are falling through*, but the leaves echo,

our plans are falling through. We are waiting
for them to hit the ground. Where is where a year ago

we lay arm in arm and heard the far-off mutter of a stream?
Where is where we loved to count the days?

The Doe

"Be careful of his mate!" you cried,
and I, the driver, veered
back to the middle of the road
and hit again the deer
another car had hit and killed
a day or two before.
                        "She doesn't know
he's dead," I said after we'd safely passed
the doe. "Her heart's the guide to her
belief."
                "No," you replied. And you'd
had your share of grief.
                        "Why else would
she wait for him like that by the
shoulder?"
                "Not for him to recover –
she's waiting for a signal that her
mourning should be over."

The Meteorite

It wouldn't be an awful way to go,
to hear the far-off whistle-tune of one
that's sailing like a hatchet toward ground.
You'd pause and turn your head to see what man
or dog had ventured near to cause the sound,
and then the rock would strike, and down you'd go.
Better than the fox who's levelled by
a hunter's gun – or men who've fought and died
by hands of men. (Others are the casualties
of time, which though it seems benign, is still
the utmost sign of our mortality.)
Some might call it droll, but surely out of all
who die, who someday also will be you
and I, a very few could claim their bullet
came from twenty thousand miles high.
I could think of harder ways by far
than to be chosen by a star, or comet-stone.

To the Lyre

after Horace Odes 1.32

My prayer: if ever in sweet idleness
and cool shade I plucked from you a song
lasting one year or many,
then let us now sing,

for you were tuned long ago in Greece
by a warrior heavy with battle and arms,
who steered his battered ship to shore
and all the while sang

of muses, appetite and wine,
of a boy forever clinging to his love,
of Lycus, his deep black eyes
and blacker hair.

Tortoise shell whose strings Apollo
played at Jupiter's feasts, my balm,
my end to endless toil, let us play again –
now's the time for song.

Peonies

On an impulse, you could eat these flowers up
the way they're floating, stemlessly, side by side
like scoops of ice cream in a crystal cup. White
and softly drizzled

with syrup (almost creeping down from the top)
and shyly turning inward still, each closed bud
leaks red along the seams and gleams like a hot
sundae. What puzzles

is how quickly these petals fan out, brown, flip,
and fray along the edges. If only they'd
stay put – if you could just keep peonies shut.
Open, they frazzle.

Notes to Poems

'These are the Happiest Days': *Cornelia and Raphael* are friends of the author.

'The Poet's Prayer': The *newly built temple* is the shrine of Apollo Citharoedus on the Palatine Hill. The ceremonial pouring of wine was a common practice at the dedication of a new temple or statue. The Liris River, dividing Latium from Campania, was known for its calm waters. Only the richest, most successful farmers used Calenian blades.

'Swiss Painters': After visiting the exhibition *Forests, Rocks, Torrents: Norwegian and Swiss Landscapes from the Lunde Collection* at the National Gallery in London. The painters described are Caspar Wolf and Alexandre Calame.

'The Chase': The first section describes a wall fragment preserved in the Palatine Museum in Rome. Several lines in section two are suggested by Ovid's Apollo and Daphne in the *Metamorphoses*.

'The Birthday': Based on Marc Chagall's painting of the same name.

'Oaks': *palsied oak* is from Robert Browning's 'Childe Roland to the Dark Tower Came'; *pent-up buds* is from Robert Frost's 'Spring Pools'.

'The Sabine Jar': *Mount Soracte* is a mountain 20 miles outside Rome.

'The Middle Way': The original addressee is thought to be Licinius Murena, a Roman politician and relative of Maecenas, Horace's patron. He was involved in a political scandal in the year preceding the publication of the *Odes*.

'A Dedication': *Diana*: goddess of the woods, hunt and childbirth. The boar's *obliquum ictum* (*sidelong thrusts*) indicate its young age.

'A Song for Lalage': The *Hydaspes* is a river of the Punjab, now called the Jhelum, where Alexander the Great defeated Porus in 326 BC. Horace and other Roman poets use it as a romantic place name.

'To the Lyre': Alcaeus, Horace's predecessor, is the Greek warrior celebrated in stanza two. Many of the odes are based upon lyrics written by Alcaeus, including Ode 1.4 (here titled 'The Sharp Cold Dissolves'). The *boy clinging to his love* is Eros; Lycus is a fictional Alcaic addressee.

Acknowledgements

I am grateful to the editors of the following publications, where some of these poems first appeared:

AGNI Online ('The Middle Way')
Ambit ('Bucket')
The American Scholar ('An Opportunity')
Ash Magazine ('To a Bull')
Eborakon ('A Song for Lalage')
The Harvard Advocate ('The Chase')
Literary Imagination ('The Fawn')
The Literary Review ('To Leuconoë', 'To the Lyre' and 'A Dedication')
Measure ('The Sharp Cold Dissolves', formerly titled 'Ode to Spring')
The New Criterion ('These Are the Happiest Days')
Parnassus: Poetry in Review ('Marine Display')
Raritan ('The Sabine Jar' and 'Simple Things are Best')
Slate ('Old Woman with a Goitre')
Southwest Review ('The Country Gambler')
The Spectator ('Peonies')
Stand ('Dragonfly' and 'An End')
The Times Literary Supplement ('Corinth')
TriQuarterly ('The Sandhill Crane')
The Yale Review ('Love Poem as Ars Poetica')

'A Dedication' also appeared on *Poetry Daily*. 'To Leuconoë' appeared on *Verse Daily* and as part of the program *Something Understood* on BBC Radio 4 and BBC World Radio.

I owe thanks to the English Department at Yale University and to the President and Fellows of Harvard College for a Radcliffe Fellowship and a George Peabody Gardner Fellowship. I have been very fortunate in my friends and teachers; I am particularly indebted to Jérôme Luc Martin, Langdon Hammer, and Jorie Graham. I am continually grateful for the support of my family, especially my husband, Bruce, whose love and encouragement has guided every step.

The Author

Erica McAlpine was born in Atlanta, Georgia. Her poems have appeared in many magazines including *The Times Literary Supplement, The Spectator, The American Scholar, The New Criterion, Ambit,* and *Slate.* She teaches literature at Keble College, Oxford, where she lives with her husband and two children. *The Country Gambler* is her first book of poems.